Collins
INTERNATIONAL PRIMARY ENGLISH

T0382088

Student's Book 2

William Collins' dream of knowledge for all began with the publication of his first book in 1819. A self-educated mill worker, he not only enriched millions of lives, but also founded a flourishing publishing house. Today, staying true to this spirit, Collins books are packed with inspiration, innovation and practical expertise. They place you at the centre of a world of possibility and give you exactly what you need to explore it.

Collins. Freedom to teach.

Published by Collins
An imprint of HarperCollins*Publishers*
The News Building
1 London Bridge Street
London SE1 9GF

Macken House, 39/40 Mayor Street Upper
Dublin 1, D01 C9W8, Ireland

Browse the complete Collins catalogue at
www.collins.co.uk

10 9 8 7

ISBN 978-0-00-836764-0

British Library Cataloguing-in-Publication Data
A catalogue record for this publication is available from the British Library.

Author: Joyce Vallar
Series editor: Daphne Paizee
Publisher: Elaine Higgleton
Product developer: Natasha Paul
Project manager: Karen Williams
Development editor: Sonya Newland
Copyeditor: Karen Williams
Proofreader: Catherine Dakin
Cover designer: Gordon MacGilp

Cover illustrator: David Roberts
Internal designer and typesetter: Ken Vail Graphic Design Ltd.
Text permissions researcher: Rachel Thorne
Image permissions researcher: Alison Prior
Illustrators: Ken Vail Graphic Design Ltd., Advocate Art, Beehive Illustration and QBS Learning
Production controller: Lyndsey Rogers
Printed in India by Multivista Global Pvt. Ltd.

Third-party websites, publications and resources referred to in this publication have not been endorsed by Cambridge Assessment International Education.

With thanks to the following teachers and schools for reviewing materials in development: Amanda DuPratt, Shreyaa Dutta Gupta, Sharmila Majumdar, Sushmita Ray and Sukanya Singhal, Calcutta International School; Akash Raut, DSB International School, Mumbai; Melissa Brobst, International School of Budapest; Shalini Reddy, Manthan International School; Taman Rama Intercultural School.

Contents

How to use this book

Key texts and images

The texts in Stage 2 provide a wide variety of different genres for learners to enjoy. The colourful illustrations provide enjoyment as well as essential support for the learners as they learn to read. Learners are introduced to stories by published authors and a variety of illustration styles.

Remember boxes

These are used to remind learners to do things that they have already learned, such as the correct use of punctuation marks.

Remember!

Items in a list are normally written one below the other. You can also write a list by separating the items in it with a comma.

Word book

These are used throughout this course. Word books allow learners to compile their own personal dictionaries which they can refer to in their writing activities. They also help learners to develop dictionary skills.

Word book

Add any new words from the story to your Word book.

Thinking time

These occur at the end of each unit in the Student's Book. Learners are encouraged to reflect on what they have read, listened to, discussed and learned.

Thinking time

Why is it important to use interesting words to describe things when you write?

1 Fun and games

Listen to the instructions. Then read the story.

Jodie the Juggler

1

Jodie loved juggling. He juggled with his socks.

He juggled with his shoes.

He juggled with three oranges and ...

2

... he broke a cup.
"Jodie," Mum said, "go outside and play football."
Jodie didn't want to play football.
He wanted to juggle.

3

He went outside and juggled with three flowerpots and ...

... the flowerpots broke!
Mum yelled, "JODIE, STOP JUGGLING!"

4 Jodie went to Asif's flat.

Hello Jodie, Come on in.

5

Jodie showed Asif how to juggle.
They juggled with Asif's socks.
They juggled with Asif's shoes.
They juggled with
three apples and ...

6

CRASH!

... they broke a plate.

7

"Boys," said Asif's dad, "go outside
and play football."
Jodie didn't want to play football.
He wanted to juggle.

8

Jodie went back down to his own flat. Mum was in the kitchen making a cake.

"No juggling!" said Mum, as Jodie picked up three eggs. But it was too late. The eggs broke!

9

"Jodie," sighed Mum, "we're going to the park to play football NOW!"

Mum carried the football. Jodie wanted to juggle.

10

Dom, Sue and Ash were in the park. They ran over to Jodie.

"Can we borrow your football?" they asked.

"Yes," said Jodie. "I don't like football. But I'll try one kick first."

11

He took the ball from Mum and kicked it as hard as he could.

Up went the ball, up and up and up.

12

Down came the ball,
down and down
and down ...

... it smashed some glass!

DANGER KEEP OUT!

Due For Demolition

13

"BRILLIANT kick!" gasped Dom.
"A golden goal!" yelled Ash.
"You're a STAR!" cried Sue.
"Jodie," said Mum firmly, "we're
going home."

14

Mum and Jodie walked
home slowly.

"Sorry, Mum," Jodie said quietly.
"Lucky that man gave us
our ball back."

Mum said, "Maybe
juggling is a good
idea. I'll make you
some juggling balls."

15

Jodie looked at her and smiled a
huge smile.

"I don't want to juggle
anymore," he said.
"I want to play
football!"

Reading and understanding

1 **See how well you understood the story. Answer the questions below.**

- What did Jodie like doing?
- What did Jodie's mother want him to do?
- What is Jodie's friend's name?
- Where did Jodie's mother take him?
- Who did Jodie meet in the park?

2 **Jodie's friends were very happy with him. Copy the sentences that tell you this.**

- They walked away.
- They smiled at Jodie.
- They had angry faces.
- They said nice things about him.
- They stood beside him.

Listening and speaking

PAIR WORK. Talk about the questions below.

1 How was Jodie's mother feeling?

2 Why was she feeling that way?

1 **Read the sentences below from the story. Who said each sentence?**

> Dom   Jodie   Ash   Asif's dad   Mum   Sue

- "JODIE, STOP JUGGLING!"
- "Boys, go outside and play football."
- "Jodie, we're going to the park to play football NOW!"
- "I don't like football."
- "BRILLIANT kick!"
- "A golden goal!"
- "You're a STAR!"
- "Jodie, we're going home."
- "I don't want to juggle any more. I want to play football!"

Hello Jodie, Come on in.

2 **Look at the first picture on page 4, after the glass was smashed. What do you think Jodie and the man said to each other?**

3 **PAIR WORK. Act out what Jodie and the man said to each other.**

Remember!
Use gestures and facial expressions, as well as words, to show how your characters feel.

Sounds and spelling

A compound word is made by combining two shorter words.

'Football' is a compound word.

foot + ball = football

1 **Join the words in the box on the left with words in the box on the right to make compound words.**

tea	butter
super	hand
up	fire
see	for
grand	

market	writing
saw	mother
fly	stairs
work	spoon
get	

2 **Use the words in the box to complete the sentences below.**

don't   could   some

- He kicked the ball as hard as he _____.
- It smashed _____ glass.
- I _____ like football.

Word book

Start a Word book. Write down words that you can use in your own writing.

Reading and writing

1 **Write a list of the things that Jodie juggled with.**

2 **Write a list of things that Jodie broke.**

3 **Write the things that Jodie did in the correct order.**

- He went to Asif's flat
- He juggled with oranges.
- He broke a plate.
- He broke the flowerpots.
- He juggled with apples.

Listening and speaking

PAIR WORK. Talk about what happened in the next part of the story.

Writing

Write what happened. Start your story with the words below.

Jodie went back ...

1 Read the title. Then look at the pictures.
What do you think this poem is about?

Janet the Juggler

Janet the juggler
Had jackets galore.
How they jingled and jangled,
Those jackets she wore.

She jiggled and juggled
With jumpers and jeans
And jam-jars and jewels
And five jelly-beans.

2 PAIR WORK. Read the poem aloud.

3 Did you enjoy this poem? Tell your partner
what you liked or did not like about it.

1 **Copy and complete the sentences. Choose from the words above.**

Word book

Write interesting words in your Word book.

- The door _____ when it opened.

- The rocket _____ into space.

- The pots and pans _____ on to the floor.

- The fire _____ as it burned.

- The girl _____ the horn on the bike.

2 **Draw a picture using each word below. Write a caption for each picture.**

Remember!

We write a caption to explain what a picture shows.

1 **Write a list of words to describe the socks in the pictures.**

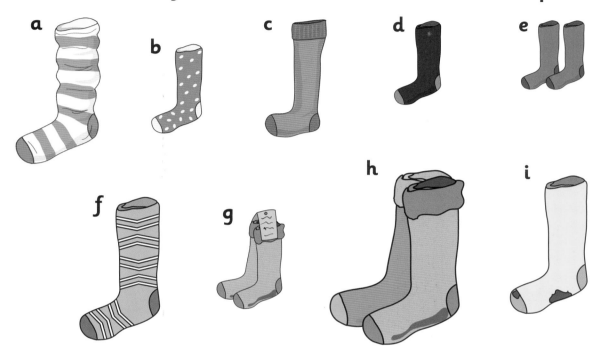

2 **Write a sentence about the socks you like the best.**

3 **Add words to make the sentences below more interesting. Copy the sentences.**

- Jodie juggled with his _____ shoes.
- "A _____ kick!" gasped Dom.
- Mum was making a _____ cake.
- "A _____ goal!" yelled Ash.
- Jodie juggled with Asif's _____ socks.

Thinking time

Why is it important to use interesting words to describe things when you write?

11

2 The Olympics

Reading

Information texts
Information texts are non-fiction.
They have headings and captions.

Read the information
below about the Olympic Games.

The Olympic Games

The First Olympic Games

The first Olympic Games were held in 776 BC in Olympia in Greece. Only men were allowed to compete. Legend has it that the winners of these ancient games were crowned with a wreath made of leaves from an olive tree.

The Modern Olympics

The first modern Olympic Games took place in 1896. The modern Olympic Games are held every four years, just as the ancient Olympic Games were held every four years at Olympia.

The summer Olympics are normally held in a leap year.

The Olympic Rings and Flag

The five Olympic rings represent the five continents of the world – America, Europe, Asia, Africa and Australia – and the coming together of athletes from different countries.

The six colours of the Olympic flag – red, yellow, green, blue and black on a white background appear on national flags around the world.

The Olympic Torch

The torch relay and the lighting of the torch in the stadium at the opening ceremony is said to keep the Olympic spirit alive all around the world.

Olympic Medals

After their events, the winners stand on the podium to get their medals. The flags of the medallists' countries are flown at the medal ceremony. The first place winner gets a gold medal, the second place gets a silver medal and the third place gets a bronze medal.

Olympic Sports

There are many different sporting events in the Olympics. Sports in the summer Olympics are different from the ones in the winter Olympics.

skiing

gymnastics

archery

Recent Olympic Games

The Olympic Games are held in countries all over the world. Cities such as Rio de Janeiro in Brazil, Paris in France, and London in the United Kingdom have hosted the games. Games have also been held in Los Angeles in the USA, in Beijing in China and in Tokyo in Japan.

Thousands of spectators travel to watch the games and millions watch the games on television.

Reading and writing

1 **Read the information on the Olympics again. Find the answers to the questions below.**

- Where were the first Olympic Games held?
- What prize did the winner of the ancient games get?
- When were the first modern Olympics?
- Which five continents do the Olympic rings represent?
- What colours make up the Olympic flag?

2 **Draw and label the flag of the country that you live in.**

3 **Find out about a flag of another country. Draw and label it.**

Word book

Add any interesting words to your Word book.

Speaking and writing

1 **PAIR WORK. Talk about what a poster for the first modern Olympic Games might have looked like.**

2 **Make a list of information for the poster.**

3 **Make a poster for the first Olympic Games.**

14

Writing

Write what is happening in each picture. Use the words in the box to help you.

medal
relay baton

javelin
diving board

high jumper
starting line

1

2

3

4

5

6

15

1 **Read the information text on pages 12 and 13 again. Then answer the questions below.**

- Name three cities in which the Olympic Games have been held.
- Name three countries in which the Olympic Games have been held.
- How do people watch the Olympic Games?
- What sports can you see during the Winter Olympics?
- What sports can you see during the Summer Olympics?

2 **PAIR WORK. Talk about the information on this poster for athletics at the Olympic Games.**

3 **Do you know what the words 'venue' and 'competitors' mean?**

4 **Make a poster to give information about a sports event at your school.**

Athletics
at the
Olympic
Games

Venue	Olympic stadium
Dates	August 1st to August 14th
Competitors	2231 (1160 men, 1071 women)

1 Look at the chart below. It has information about
Olympic medal winners.

Country		Gold medals	Silver medals	Bronze medals
Ethiopia		22	11	21
Jamaica		22	35	21
France		212	241	263
Japan		142	136	161
Finland		101	85	117
Brazil		30	36	63

2 **Write the name of the country for each flag.**

a

b

c

d

e

f

| Brazil |
| Jamaica |
| Ethiopia |
| Japan |
| France |
| Finland |

3 **Read the table on page 17 again. Then answer the questions below.**

- Which country on this list won the most gold medals?

- How many silver medals did Japan win?

- How many bronze medals did Finland win?

- Which countries have the same number of gold medals?

- Who has more silver medals, Brazil or Jamaica?

Reading and writing

1 **Read the chart. Then answer the questions below.**

- Who won the men's 110 metre hurdles?
- What was his time?
- Who ran the race in 13.17 seconds?
- Which country did the bronze medallist come from?

Men's 110 metre hurdles			
🥇1	Omar McLeod	13.05 seconds	JAM
🥈2	Orlando Ortega	13.17 seconds	SPA
🥉3	Dimitri Bascou	13.24 seconds	FRA

2 **Imagine you are an Olympic athlete. Write in your diary after your event.**

Write about:

- how you felt before the race as you waited at the starting line.
- how you felt after the race.
- the crowd's reaction.
- your time.
- how you felt on the podium.

Usain Bolt

Usain Bolt was born in Jamaica on 21 August 1986. He was one of the fastest sprinters in the world before he retired. He held records for the 100 and 200 metre events for many years. He is so fast he has been given the nickname 'Lightning Bolt'.

He won three gold medals at the 2012 Olympic Games in London, UK.

He defended all three titles at the 2016 Olympic Games in Rio de Janeiro, by winning gold in the 100 metres, 200 metres and 4 × 100 metres relay.

❶ Answer the questions below.

- When was Usain Bolt born?
- Where was Usain Bolt born?
- What is Usain Bolt's nickname?
- How many gold medals did he win at the 2012 London Olympics?
- How many gold medals did he win at the 2016 Rio de Janeiro Olympics?

❷ Write a short article for your local newspaper about Usain Bolt's win at the 2016 Olympics.

- Think of a good headline for your article.

Thinking time

Talk about the fiction and non-fiction texts you have read. Which one did you find easier to read? Why?

3 Creatures great and small

Reading and speaking

Look at the pictures and talk about the questions. Then read the story.

- What is the story about?
- Where does the story take place?
- Who is the main character in the story?

> **Traditional tales**
>
> Traditional stories:
> - may come from different parts of the world.
> - are usually old.
> - were often spoken rather than written down.

The Ugly Duckling

❶

A long time ago, on a farm, a mother duck sat on her eggs, waiting for them to hatch.

One, two, three yellow ducklings came out of the shells.

One more egg still had to hatch. CRACK! CRACK! CRACK! Out came a rather different looking duckling.

❷

Mother duck led her children to a nearby pond. First the three fluffy, yellow ducklings and then the scruffy brown one. He didn't look much like a duckling at all!

Mother duck began to teach the ducklings to swim. But the yellow ducklings did not want the scruffy duckling to join in. They said he was too ugly.

The ugly duckling got out of the water.
Mother duck was cross with him.
The ugly duckling was sad.

The ugly duckling wandered off around
the farm. He felt alone. All the farm
animals stared at him.

The cows mooed, the geese cackled and
the hens clucked. The ugly duckling felt
very frightened and ran way.

The geese chased the
ugly duckling back to
the pond.

7

The ugly duckling was all alone. "No one wants me," he said. He stayed at the pond for a long time. The weather began to change and the leaves fell from the trees.

8

The weather grew colder, wetter and windier. One day the ugly duckling looked up and saw two large birds flying across the sky.

"I wonder where they are going," he thought as he gazed up at the sky. The two large birds kept on flying.

9

Winter set in and the lonely duckling spent his days trying to keep warm. He was growing bigger and one day he noticed that some of his feathers were falling out too.

10

Slowly more feathers fell out and others grew in their place. The new feathers were a different colour.

Stop reading here. In pairs talk about how you think the story will end. Explain why you think this.

The weather began to change. It became warmer and leaves grew on the trees. The sun was shining. The ugly duckling looked down and saw a reflection in the water.

"What is this? Why is it so close to me?" he asked.

He stretched his neck and the bird stretched its neck too. Suddenly, he knew what had happened. He was not a duck at all. He was a beautiful swan.

Next day he met another beautiful swan just like him, and they swam through the water. A group of ducks looked on in amazement. Every day the beautiful swan and his friend swam in the pond where he first learned to swim.

Reading and writing

1 **Answer the questions below.**

- How many eggs hatched?
- How many ducklings were yellow?
- What did mother duck teach the ducklings?
- Where did the ugly duckling wander off to?
- Who chased the ugly duckling back to the pond?
- What did ugly duckling see in the sky?

Remember!

If you do not understand any parts of the story, ask a partner or your teacher what they mean.

2 **Read the sentences below. Copy the sentences that are true.**

- The yellow ducklings wanted to swim with the ugly duckling.
- All the farm animals stared at the ugly duckling.
- The geese chased the ugly duckling back to the pond.
- The reflection in the water was of a swan.
- The swan lived with his friend on a different pond.

3 **PAIR WORK. Talk about the different types of weather in the story.**

4 **Write a sentence about each picture.**

Reading, writing and speaking

Read the story again.

- Write down any words that you don't know.
- Talk about the words with a partner to work out their meaning.

Word book

Write any new words in your Word book.

Reading and writing

① **Read the words in the box. Find the words in the story.**

mooed   cackled   clucked

② **Copy and complete the sentences below.**

- The hens _____ as the farmer fed them.
- The cows _____ when they were being milked.
- The goose _____ when she laid an egg.

③ **Write the answers to the questions below.**

- Who said this?

  "No one wants me."

- Who might have said these words?

  "It is time to learn to swim."

  "We don't want to play with you."

  "I feel very frightened."

  "I want to be your friend."

④ **Write a sentence using one of the words from the box in activity 1 above.**

26

Sounds and spelling

PAIR WORK. What is the plural of each of these words? Say the words.

goose   man   woman   child   foot   person

Remember!

We add –s or –es to make plural forms of most nouns, but some nouns are different.

Speaking, listening and writing

1 PAIR WORK. Talk about the setting of the story.

2 Pretend you are one of the other animals in the story. Tell your partner what you saw. The pictures will help.

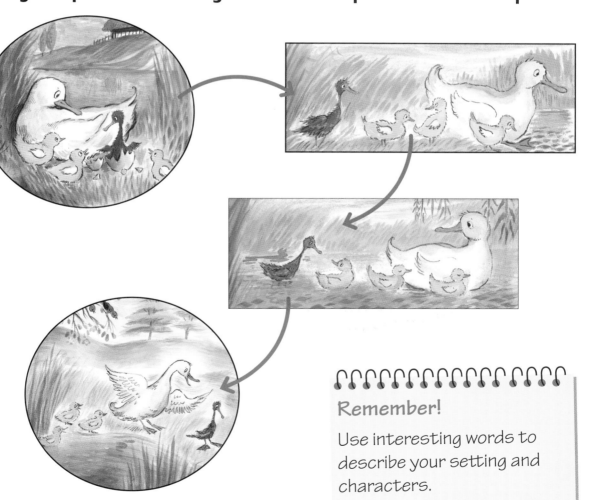

Remember!

Use interesting words to describe your setting and characters.

Reading and writing

Read the sentences below. Write the sentences that are true.

- Farm animals live in the wild.
- Some farm animals graze in fields.
- Farm animals can provide food.
- An elephant is a farm animal.
- Vets look after farm animals.

Speaking, reading and writing

❶ PAIR WORK. Choose a farm animal to research.

❷ Draw and label a picture of your farm animal.

❸ Write five interesting facts about your farm animal.

Remember!

When talking with a partner:

- Take turns to speak.
- Try to say something different each time.
- Listen carefully when your partner is speaking.

❹ Give a short presentation to the class about your farm animal.

Reading and writing

Do you think a swan or a duck would be a good pet? Read the words in the box. Copy the headings and write the animal names in two lists.

Animals we can keep as pets	Animals we should not keep as pets

duck mouse fox
horse tiger
elephant goldfish
rabbit cat
swan hamster

Speaking and listening

PAIR WORK. Talk about the questions below.

- What would a pet animal need?
- How would you look after a pet animal?

Writing

You have asked a friend to look after your pet for a short time. Write a note telling your friend what they will need to do.

You could use some of the sentence openings below.
- In the morning ...
- After school ...
- At the weekend ...

29

1 Read the two poems silently on your own.

2 Tell your partner which poem you like best and why.

Caterpillar

Creepy crawly caterpillar
Looping up and down,
Furry tufts of hair along
Your back of golden brown.

You will soon be wrapped in silk,
Asleep for many a day;
And then, a handsome butterfly,
You'll stretch and fly away.

By Mary Dawson

The Caterpillar

Brown and furry
Caterpillar in a hurry;
Take your walk
To the shady leaf or stalk.

May no toad spy you,
May the little birds pass by you;
Spin and die,
To live again a butterfly.

By Christina Georgina Rosetti

Writing

1 Make a list of all the words the poets used to describe caterpillars.

2 Read the poems again. Find the words that rhyme with each word below.

- 'down' rhymes with _____

- 'die' rhymes with _____

- 'walk' rhymes with _____

- 'day' rhymes with _____

Remember!

When the endings of words sound the same, we say the words rhyme.

1 **Look at the pictures. Write the words.**

2 **Copy and complete the sentences. Use the correct word from the box.**

to   too

- The ground is _____ wet _____ dig.
- What does a duck like _____ eat?
- We go _____ school on a bus.
- It is _____ hot _____ play outside.
- He is _____ small _____ reach the peg.

3 **Copy and complete the sentences below.**

- It is _____ hot in the sun.
- A swan has _____ wings.
- I went _____ play in the park.
- The box is _____ heavy _____ carry.
- There are _____ cakes left on the plate.

Thinking time

Talk about how you work out meanings of new words when you are reading.

two swans

4 *Kind Emma*

1 **Look at the pictures. What do you think this story will be about?**

2 **Talk about the two characters that you can see in the pictures. Then read the text.**

Kind Emma lived all alone with no one to talk to.

One night, a little voice called,
"Oh, dear Emma, oh!
Where can I go
in the wind and in the snow?"

"Come into my house," said Kind Emma.
She opened the door and a tiny thing scuttled in.
It was almost too small to be seen.

Then the little voice said:
"Oh, dear Emma, oh!
Your fire has burned low
And I shiver so!"

"I'll make the fire glow for you," said Kind Emma,
and she poked the fire.

Then the little voice said:
"Oh, dear Emma, oh!
I ate long ago.
I need food so!"

"You can share what I have," said Kind Emma.

She put a dish of hot soup and a very small spoon on the table.
The tiny thing stayed hidden. It was afraid to come out.

"Goodnight!" said Kind Emma. She hoped the tiny thing would
come out and eat if she left the room.

Next morning, when Emma awoke ...

Stop reading here. In pairs, talk about how you
think the story will end. Now read on.

... the fire burned and the water was hot. Fresh bread was ready.
The floor was scrubbed and the house was tidy and clean.

"Good food and a fire, and someone to
talk to! What more could I want?"
said Kind Emma.
The tiny thing stayed with Kind Emma
for all of the rest of her days.

Reading and writing

1 Read the story again.
Write the names of the
characters in the story.

2 Choose the correct words to complete
the sentences below. Copy the sentences.

scuttled   lived   stayed   poked   put   was

- Kind Emma _____ all alone.
- A tiny thing _____ in through the door.
- Kind Emma _____ the fire.
- She _____ a dish of hot soup on the table.
- The tiny thing _____ hidden.
- It _____ afraid to come out.

3 Write a sentence using 'and' to
tell what Emma did next.

4 Write the names of the people
who live in your house.

5 Write a sentence about your house.

6 Write your name and address.

34

Reading and writing

1 Write the answers to the questions below. Remember to answer in sentences.

- Who scuttled in when Emma opened the door?
- What did Emma put on the table?

2 Write the sentences that tell that Emma was kind.

- You can share what I have.
- Kind Emma lived all alone.
- I'll make the fire glow for you.
- When I awoke the house was clean.
- Come into my house.

Listening and speaking

PAIR WORK. Talk about a time when you were kind to someone.

Writing

1 Write about a time when you were kind to someone. Remember to tell:

- the person's name.
- whether they were a friend, a relative or someone that you had just met.
- what the kind thing was that you did.

2 PAIR WORK. Read your stories to each other. What do you like about each other's stories?

1 **Who did the things below? Was it Emma or the 'thing'?**

Make two lists. One for Emma and one for the 'thing'.

- opened the door
- scuttled in
- poked the fire
- stayed hidden
- scrubbed the floor
- left the room
- stayed with Kind Emma

2 **Write the verbs from question 1 in a list.**

3 **Read the words in the first box. Find words in the second box that have a similar meaning. Write them.**

shiver	scuttle	glow	poke	share

Word book

Write interesting words in your Word book.

run quickly

push a pointed object into someone or something

shake slightly because you feel cold or ill

shine brightly

divide things

For example: share – to divide things.

1 **Read the sentences below about the story.
Write 'true', 'false' or 'can't tell' for each one.**

- Kind Emma lives alone.
- Kind Emma has a sister.
- Kind Emma has a table in her house.
- Kind Emma lives in a house with no stairs.
- Kind Emma didn't have a fire in the house.
- Kind Emma put a dish of hot soup on the table.
- Kind Emma likes baking cakes.

2 **Copy and complete the sentences below.**

unwell	unlock	dislike
unfit	unpack	disobey

- He used a key to _____ the door.
- We had to _____ the suitcase after our holiday.
- The player should not _____ the rules of the game.
- I stayed in bed when I was feeling _____.
- The runner was _____ for the race.
- I _____ some vegetables.

Reading and writing

1 **Write the names of the days of the week.**

2 **Write two diary pages for Emma. Write the sentences below in the correct pages.**

- When I awoke the house was tidy and clean.
- I was lonely.
- A tiny 'thing' came into my house.
- There was fresh bread on the table.
- I gave it a dish of hot soup.
- I said goodnight and went to bed.
- I had someone to talk to.

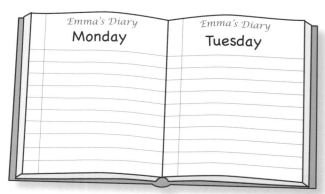

Emma's Diary
Monday

Emma's Diary
Tuesday

3 **Think of five things that you do in a school day.**

- Draw each of the five things in order.
- Write a caption under each picture.

Writing and speaking

1 **Write what is happening in each picture.**

2 **What happened next?**
Complete the story.

Next morning, when Emma awoke ...

Remember!
- Use joining words in your sentences: 'and', 'but', 'or', 'because', 'when'.
- Choose interesting words for your story.

3 **PAIR WORK. Talk about a different ending for the story.**

4 **Write a different ending for the story.**

Next morning, when Emma awoke ...

Reading and writing

PAIR WORK.

1 **Answer the questions below.**

- Where did Emma meet the 'thing'?
- How did it feel?
- How did Emma try to help?
- What happened next?

2 **Pretend that you met a 'thing'. Plan a story.**

Think about:

> where you met the 'thing'.

↓

> what happened when you met.

↓

> what your 'thing' looked like.

↓

> how you helped the 'thing'.

↓

> what happened next.

3 **Write your story. Read it aloud. Correct any mistakes.**

Thinking time

What did you think of this story? What message do you think it has? Would you choose to read this kind of story? Why, or why not?

5 Animals and us

Listening and speaking

① **Listen as your teacher reads the first two verses from this poem.**

② **Talk about the title of the poem. Why do you think it is called _Dolphin Ballet_?**

Dolphin Ballet

A graceful water weaving dolphin
swirls wakes of gentle waves –
a white, silver blue phantom
shimmering in the noonday sun.

Piercing the surface,
she dances an aquatic ballet
of corkscrew pirouettes
and majestic somersaults.

By Robert Charles Howard

Reading and speaking

This is the title page of the story you are going to read.

① What type of story is this?

② What do you think the story will be about?

③ Now read the story on pages 42 to 43.

Remember!
Stories such as folk tales were often written long ago and may come from different parts of the world.

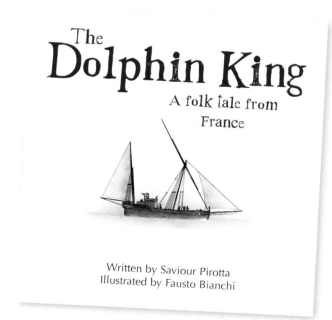

The
Dolphin King
A folk tale from
France

Written by Saviour Pirotta
Illustrated by Fausto Bianchi

The Dolphin King

1 Jean and his friends were fishermen.

Jean said, "I can throw a spear better than any of you."

He hurled his spear at a dolphin.

The animal screamed and dived beneath the waves.

2 Suddenly, a fierce storm blew up and it looked as though the boat might sink.

Then Jean and his friends saw a strange knight rising out of the waves.

The knight shouted, "You nearly killed the dolphin king, and for this you'll all drown!"

3 Jean cried, "No, I alone threw the spear. Take me."

The knight carried Jean down to the bottom of the sea.

There, the dolphin king was waiting.

The knight whispered to Jean, "You must heal him."

4 Gently, Jean removed the spear. He cleaned the wound.

The king opened his eyes and said, "Promise me that you and your friends will never hunt dolphins again."

Jean cried, "I promise."

5 The knight took him back to the boat. The storm had died and Jean's friends were saved.

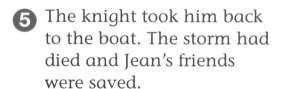

Word book

Write interesting words from the story in your Word book.

1 **Answer the questions below.**

- What work did Jean do?
- What did Jean use to catch fish?

2 **Read the sentences below about the story. Answer 'true', 'false' or 'can't tell' for each one.**

- Jean went fishing with his friends.
- Jean went fishing on Monday.
- Jean was boastful.
- Jean's friend hurled his spear.
- Jean's spear hit a dolphin.

3 **Copy the sentence below that tells what happened next after Jean hurled his spear.**

- The dolphin swam away.
- The dolphin screamed and dived beneath the waves.

4 **Write a sentence that tells you Jean was boastful.**

5 **Write a sentence that tells the reader about the story setting.**

1 **Copy and complete the sentences below. Use the words in the box.**

strange   hurled   heal   fierce   removed   whispered

- Jean _____ his spear at a dolphin.
- Suddenly a _____ storm blew up.
- Jean and his friends saw a _____ knight.
- The knight _____ to Jean, "You must heal him."
- Gently, Jean _____ the spear.

Word book

Write tricky words in your Word book.

2 **Write the word that tells you:**

- the storm started very quickly.
- Jean was very careful when he removed the spear.

3 **Write a sentence to tell when the knight shouted.**

4 **Write a sentence to tell when the knight whispered.**

5 **Write a sentence with the word 'shouted' and a sentence with the word 'whispered'.**

The knight shouted …

The knight whispered …

Reading and writing

1 **Who said it? Write the name.**

> Jean   the dolphin king   the knight

- "I can throw a spear better than any of you."
- "You nearly killed the dolphin king, and for this you'll all drown!"
- "No, I alone threw the spear. Take me."
- "You must heal him."
- "Promise me that you and your friends will never hunt dolphins again."
- "I promise."

2 **Write what happened next in the story.**

3 **Write the words from the box that describe Jean after the storm blew up.**

> afraid   brave   honest   fearful   fearless   truthful   dishonest

Speaking and listening

GROUP WORK. Talk about the questions below.

1 Do you think Jean kept his promise?

2 Why you think Jean did this?

Sounds and spelling

1 **Write the words from the box that end in –ear.**

fear	dear	deal	hear	near
heal	clear	spear	clean	shear

2 **Copy and complete the sentences.**
Use words from question 1.

- You can see the fish in the _____ water.
- My house is _____ the school.
- I cannot _____ what you are saying.

3 **Write the words from the box that end in –air.**

chair	chain	fair	hair
stain	stair	pair	pain

4 **Write words that sound the same but have a different spelling.**

- dear _____
- hair _____
- stare _____
- pear _____.

5 **Choose one pair of words. Write a sentence for each word.**

Reading and writing

1 **Read the words about different types of weather.
Write the ones that might happen in a fierce storm.**

gentle breeze	heavy rain	high waves
showers	calm sea	strong winds
bright sunshine	dark clouds	downpours
fluffy clouds	thunder and lightning	blue sky

2 **Write a story about being caught
in a storm.**

- Where were you?
- What did you do during the storm?
- What happened after the storm?

Word book

Write new words
in your Word book.
Try to use the words
in your story.

The story is in three parts.
Beginning – before Jean threw the spear.
Middle – what happened after he threw the spear.
End – what happened after Jean made a promise.

1 **Write the sentences below under the correct headings.**

beginning   middle   end

- The knight carried Jean down to the bottom of the sea.
- The knight took him back to the boat.
- Jean hurled a spear.
- The storm died down.
- Jean removed the spear.
- The dolphin dived beneath the waves.
- Jean and his friends were fishing.

2 **What did Jean promise to do?**

3 **Write the words below that best describe a promise.**

- something that you might be able to do
- something that you will do

4 **PAIR WORK. Talk about the questions below.**

- What things have you promised to do?
- Do you always keep your promise?
- What happens if you make a promise and you don't keep it?

Reading

Read the text about dolphins. Is this a fiction or non-fiction text?

Listening and speaking

Talk about:

- the different ways that humans can harm dolphins.
- how oil can injure or kill dolphins.

Writing

Make a poster about a class event to raise money to help dolphins.

Thinking time

Did you take turns and give information when you spoke with your partner about dolphins?

Dolphins

Dolphins are mammals that live in the ocean.

They are often injured or even killed by humans. Sometimes they get tangled in fishing nets. Sometimes they are killed for food or bait.

The most serious threat to dolphins is pollution.

Oil spills caused by underwater drilling or a ship running aground can cause dolphins to die.

- Oil can cover the dolphin's blowhole and enter its lungs, making it difficult to breathe.
- Oil can get into the dolphin's eyes, causing damage and even blindness.
- Oil can enter the dolphin's mouth. The dolphin can swallow it and damage its internal organs.

6 Staying safe

Read the contents page. Then answer the questions below.

World's Deadliest Creatures

Written by Anna Claybourne

Contents

- What will you find out about in this book?
- What is the title of the book?
- What kind of book is it?
- Who wrote the book?
- There is no illustrator's name. Why do you think this is?
- What will you find out about on page 6?
- What will you find out about on page 10?
- On which pages will you find out about staying safe?

Look at the pictures and read the information on pages 52 to 54.

❷ Deadly or not?

golden poison dart frog

dangerous!

whale shark

❸

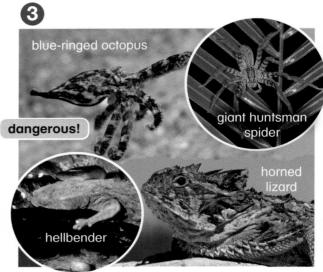

blue-ringed octopus

dangerous!

giant huntsman spider

horned lizard

hellbender

Which are the deadliest creatures in the world? Some look dangerous, but they are not. Others look safe, but watch out!

❹ Venomous fangs

Found in:
Australia

This funnel-web spider has deadly **venom** in its big fangs.
It can even bite through soft shoes.

❺

Found in:
African countries
China
India

A spitting cobra can spit its venom two metres. It aims venom at your eyes, which can cause blindness.

⑥ Nasty stings

Found in:
Middle Eastern countries
North African countries

Deathstalker scorpions
hide in dark places.
They sting with their tails.

⑦

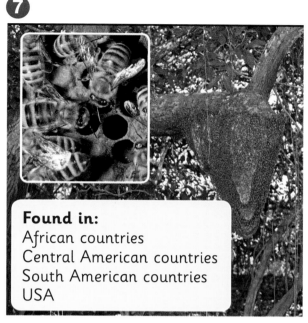

Found in:
African countries
Central American countries
South American countries
USA

Over 20000 killer bees can
swarm together.
Each bee has a very sharp sting.

⑧ Deadly in the water

Found in:
Seas around:
Australia
Japan

The blue-ringed octopus
has a venomous beak.
Its bite is deadly.

⑨

Found in:
Seas around:
African countries
Australia
Central American countries
India
South American countries

Tiger sharks often swim close
to beaches, so sometimes they
attack humans.
Their teeth and jaws are strong
enough to bite you in half.

10 Deadliest poison

Found in:
Seas around:
Australia
Japan

The box jellyfish has long, venomous **tentacles**.
Its venom can kill a human in three minutes.

11

Found in:
South American countries

The most **poisonous** creature in the world is the golden poison dart frog. It's deadly to eat, or even to touch.

12 Stay safe!

If you see a dangerous animal like the ones in this book, keep away.

13

Most animals will **not** attack you, unless you bother them.
Always treat animals with respect.

**Read the pages below.
Then answer the questions.**

Page 2

- Which creature is dangerous?
- Which creature is not dangerous? How can you tell?

Page 3

- Which creature is labelled 'dangerous'?

Page 4

- How does the funnel-web spider kill its prey?
- In what country is the funnel-web spider found?

Page 5

- How could a spitting cobra hurt you?
- In what countries are spitting cobras found?

Page 6

- How could a scorpion hurt you?
- In what countries are deathstalker scorpions found?
- Where do deathstalker scorpions hide?

Page 7

- What is a swarm of bees?
- How many killer bees can be in a swarm?
- In what countries are killer bees found?

Reading and writing

1 Read pages 52 to 54 again to find out about dangerous creatures that live in water.

2 Copy and complete the sentences below.

tiger shark

blue-ringed octopus

box jellyfish

- The _____ has a venomous beak.
- The _____ sometimes attacks humans.
- The _____ has long venomous tentacles.

Speaking and listening

PAIR WORK. Talk about why people need water.

Writing

1 Write three things that people need water for.

2 Draw a picture to show one thing that people need water for. Write a caption under it.

Remember!
Write the question *What do people need water for?* Then write your three things in sentences underneath.

Use words such as 'some', 'most' and 'all' in your sentences.

Reading and writing

	bites	spits	stings
spider	✓		
cobra		✓	
scorpion			✓
octopus	✓		
bee			✓
shark	✓		

1 Read the chart to find the answers.

- Does a cobra bite, spit or sting?
- Which creatures bite their prey?
- Which creatures sting their prey?

2 Think about the dangerous creatures you have read about. Write a list of dangerous animals.

3 Write a list of animals that are not dangerous.

Speaking and listening

Use books or the internet to find out about a different deadly animal. Give a presentation to the class.

- Say why you chose that animal.
- Say what is deadly about it.
- Talk about each other's presentations. What did you like and why?

Sounds and spelling

1 Add the missing syllable to each word. Copy the sentences.

- The funnel-web spi_____ has venom in its fangs.
- The spitting cob_____ can spit its venom two metres.
- The scor__on stings with its tail.
- The oc_____pus has a venomous beak.
- The box jel__fish has long tentacles.

com/pu/ter

2 Add the missing syllable to complete each month. Write the names of the months.

Jan/__/ar/y

Feb/ru/__/y

_____

Ap/_____

_____

_____

Ju/_____

Au/_____

Sep/_____/ber

Oc/to/_____

___/vem/ber

De/_____/ber

1 **Write the words in rhyming groups under each heading.**

head   bear   beach   thread   tear
teach   reach   read   wear

sounds like 'peach'   sounds like 'bread'   sounds like 'pear'

Listening and speaking

PAIR WORK. Read the sentences in the box. Talk about:

- the underlined words in the sentences.
- how you know how to say each underlined word.

The black car is in the <u>lead</u> in the race.
I <u>read</u> my library book last night.

Sounds and spelling

Use the underlined words in the box to complete the rhymes. Write the rhymes.

1 _____ rhymes with head.

2 _____ rhymes with bead.

1 **PAIR WORK.**
Talk about the pictures.

a

b

c
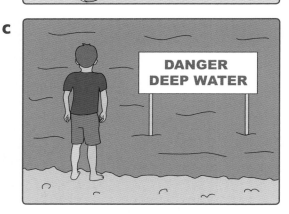

d

DANGER
KEEP OUT

e

BEWARE
FALLING ROCKS

DANGER
DEEP WATER

f

2 **Write sentences to tell about the dangers shown in each picture.**

Thinking time

What safety issues do you come across in your everyday life? As well as dangers you can see in the pictures, think about dangers you cannot see, such as safety when someone is using the internet. How can they stay safe online?

7 *If*

Reading

If is a story poem. Read the poem. As you read, think about patterns such as repeated words and rhymes.

Story poems

Story poems are longer poems. Rhymes and words are often repeated in story poems.

If is a poem that tries to tell the reader how to cope on days when they wake up and everything around them seems to go wrong. The writer uses their imagination to show what this might feel like.

For example:

What do you think is happening in the first picture? What might the boy not want to do?

Would alligators really be in a boy's bedroom?

Would a hippo really be eating his food?

1

If you can keep your head when alligators
are stealing all the bedclothes from your bed
and keep your cool when, 15 minutes later,
a greedy hippo eats your eggy bread …

2

If you can walk to school with your big brother
although he really is a dreadful sight,
and wave goodbye, although your lovely mother
has turned into a monster overnight …

3

If you can cross the playground in the morning –
a playground full of fearsome dinosaurs –
and keep on walking when, without a warning,
they raise their heads and roar and roar and roar …

4

If you can stand and watch a spaceship landing
and when the others run away in fright,
you treat the strange green men with understanding
and though they're rude, you are still polite …

5

If you can count to ten while angry rhinos
are grunting (just because they can't do sums)
and say, "I'll teach you everything that I know
but quick – before the dragon teacher comes …"

6

If you can play at baseball with a cheetah
who, fast as lightning, runs from base to base
and even though you know you'll never beat her,
you somehow keep a smile upon your face,

7

Then you will see that they're just human beings
with hopes and worries much the same as you.
Despite their snatch and grab and disagreeing
there's lots of lovely things they also do.

If you can see all this and never doubt it
(though crocodiles will eat your cheesy snack)
you'll love the world and everything about it
and – what is more – the world will love you back.

8

Everyone's a monster

We're all human beings.

Reading and writing

Read the poem again. Answer the questions below.

- Who is the main character in the poem?
- Write the names of five other characters in the poem.
- Where was the boy at the start of the poem?
- Who walked to school with the boy?
- Where did the boy meet the dinosaurs?
- How did the strange green men travel?
- What animals can't do sums?

Speaking and listening

PAIR WORK. Talk about the questions below.

- Who might be stealing the bedclothes?
- Who might be eating the eggy bread?
- Why might the boy think his brother was a dreadful sight?
- Have you ever been called a 'monster'?
- Do you know why?
- What did you do to change?

Remember!

When you are talking about a topic:
- take turns.
- speak clearly.
- look at your partner.
- listen carefully.

Spelling: suffixes

A suffix is a set of letters added to the end of a word.

For example:

Your love**ly** mother has turned into a monster overnight.

love + **ly** = lovely

–*ly* is a suffix.

1 **Add the suffix –*ly* to change each word.**

smart + ly	quick + ly	lone + ly
slow + ly	calm + ly	like + ly
friend + ly	smooth + ly	safe + ly
bright + ly	loud + ly	nice + ly

2 **Copy and complete the sentences with the correct word.**

- The car drove _____ along the street. (slow, slowly)
- The car is very _____. (slow, slowly)
- I hope you have a _____ journey. (safe, safely)
- He crossed the road _____. (safe, safely)
- She is a good _____. (friendly, friend)
- He is a _____ boy. (friendly, friend)

3 **Choose two words from question 1 and write a sentence with each one.**

1 **Copy and complete the sentences.**

- Matilda is _____ than Anna.
- Anna is _____ than Matilda.

- Clare is the _____.
- Dan is the _____.

2 **Write four sentences with the words in the box.**

heaviest smallest heavier taller

Word book

Add three words from question 3 to your Word book.

3 **Which words in the box have the suffix –er?**

winter   faster   longer   summer
answer   stronger   bigger   wetter

4 **Write a sentence with one of the words where –er is NOT a suffix.**

5 **Copy and complete each sentence with the correct verb.**

- He _____ to school every day. (walks, walking)
- They all _____ at the joke. (laughing, laugh)
- The twins are _____ a birthday card to their Grandma. (sends, sending)
- We _____ football with our friends. (plays, played)
- Sam is _____ fast to catch the bus. (running, runs)

1 **Read the sentences below. Write the nouns, verbs and adjectives from the sentences in three lists.**

Nouns	Verbs	Adjectives
alligators		

- When alligators are stealing all the bedclothes.
- A greedy hippo eats your eggy bread.
- Your lovely mother has turned into a monster.

2 **Copy and complete each sentence below with adjectives.**

- When _____ alligators are stealing all the _____ bedclothes.
- When _____ hippos eat my _____ toast.
- When _____ dinosaurs are in the _____ playground.
- When _____ men come in a _____ spaceship.

3 **Write an interesting sentence with at least one noun, one verb and one adjective. Use 'some', 'most' or 'all' in your sentence.**

Reading and speaking

Read the poem on pages 61 to 63 again.

- Choose your favourite verse.
- Learn the verse.
- Work in groups to prepare and give a performance of it.

Writing

Imagine you have a dinosaur for a pet. You are going to write a story about it.

1 Draw a picture of you and your dinosaur.

2 Plan your writing. Imagine taking your dinosaur to the park.

- What did you do in the park?
- What might have happened?
- What might someone in the park have said?

3 Write your story. Join ideas with words like 'and', 'but' and 'because'. Think about punctuation.

Remember!

- Use interesting adjectives to describe the dinosaur and the park, such as 'enormous', 'gigantic', 'play', 'local'.
- Use direct speech – the actual words someone said. Put the words in speech marks (" ").

Sounds and spelling

1 Read the verse below from the poem. Write the words that rhyme. What do you notice about the rhyming words?

If you can play at baseball with a cheetah
who, fast as lightning, runs from base to base
and even though you know you'll never beat her,
you somehow keep a smile upon your face

2 Use the letters in the box to make rhyming words. Write the rhyming words in a list.

d r m p n l tr pl pr tw sl

face	mice

3 Choose two words, one from each list. Write two sentences using the words.

4 Copy the words in the box. Circle the soft 'c' in each word.

Circus   circle   bicycle   cereal
cinema   city   stencil   December

Writing and speaking

1 Imagine you are a reporter from a newspaper. You interview the boy from the poem *If*. Write three questions you would ask him.

2 PAIR WORK. Role-play the interview with the boy. Take turns to be the boy from the story and the reporter.

A reporter interviews people.

Reading and writing

Write a newspaper report for your local newspaper about the boy's experiences.

- Write a headline first.
- In your first sentence, say who you interviewed.
- In your second sentence, say what you asked the boy about.
- Then write what the boy told you.
- Write an ending to the report.

Remember!

When writing your article, ask these questions:
- Who was involved?
- What happened?
- When did it happen?
- Where did it happen?
- What is happening now?

Thinking time

Did the interview help you to write your newspaper article? What other questions could you have asked?

8 *The Pot of Gold*

Speaking and reading

PAIR WORK.

❶ Look at the front cover of the book. Talk about:

- the characters' appearance.
- how you think they are feeling.
- what they are wearing.
- any other information you can get from the front cover.

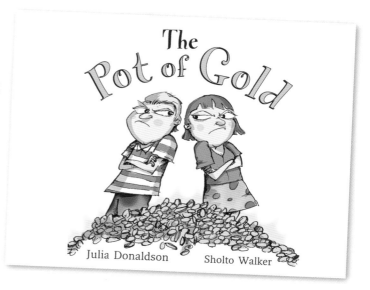

❷ Read the 'blurb' from the back cover of the book. Talk about the questions below.

- What do you think is going to happen in the story?
- What part might the little man have in the story?

Sandy and Bonny
were always arguing
and nothing ever went right for them.
But one day a little man came to stay.
Would he really change their luck?

❸ Now take turns to read the story.

The Pot of Gold

1

Sandy and Bonny kept sheep.

"Too many sheep," said Bonny.

"Not enough sheep," said Sandy.

The two of them were always arguing.

2

One evening, they were busy arguing when there was a tap at the door. There on the doorstep stood a little man. He wore a green hat and a ragged green coat. His green shoes had holes in the toes.

3

"Can I stay here for two nights?" he asked.

"Yes," said Sandy.

"No," said Bonny.

"I can pay," said the little man. He took two gold coins out of his pocket.

"Well?" he asked. "Can I stay?"

4

"Yes!" said Sandy and Bonny. For once they agreed about something.

They took him to his room.

"Good night, and good luck!" said the little man. Bonny laughed. "We never have any luck," she said. But she was wrong.

5

The next day, Sandy was on the hill with the sheep when he saw a big pile of stones.

"That's funny," he said. "I can see something gleaming."

Sandy took away some of the stones, and he saw a heap of gold coins!

"I'll run home and fetch a big pot to carry them in," he said.

6

He started to run down the hill. But then he stopped.

"Suppose someone finds the coins when I'm gone?" he said to himself.

He put the stones back and stuck his stick into them, so that he would be able to find the right place again.

7

Sandy ran home. "We're rich!" he shouted. "Don't be so silly," said Bonny. But then Sandy told her about the gold coins. He grabbed a pot. "Let's go and get them!" he said.

8

"Don't be so silly," said Bonny again. "People will see us. Then everyone will want some of the gold."

"That's true," said Sandy. "Let's wait till it's dark."

9

Bonny put some food and water on the table.

"Just think," she said. "With all that money we can buy a new house."

"Don't be silly," said Sandy. "We don't need a new house. But we do need some more sheep."

10

"Sheep!" cried Bonny. "We've got too many sheep already. We can stop keeping sheep. And I can buy lots of new clothes."

"Clothes!" shouted Sandy. "You don't need any more clothes! You've got too many clothes already!"

He banged his fist on the table.

"I have not!" yelled Bonny. And she threw a chip at him.

"Missed!" shouted Sandy, and he threw some beans at her.

11

They were shouting so loudly that they didn't hear the little man come downstairs.

"Please could you stop making so much noise?" he asked.

12

"Oh, shut up!" yelled Bonny.

She was in such a bad mood that she picked up a jug of water and threw it all over the little man.

Sandy laughed.

The little man gave them both a funny look. Then he went upstairs.

"Good night," he said. But this time he didn't say, "Good luck".

"No, I wasn't!" Sandy shouted. "I really did find a heap of gold coins." Then he spotted another pile of stones with a stick. "That's funny," he said.

Sandy and Bonny looked around them. There were hundreds of piles of stones, each one with a stick in it.

They hunted all night, but they didn't find the gold.

It was dark now and the moon was out. "Let's go and get the gold," said Sandy. They took the pot and carried it up the hill.

"There's the pile of stones with your stick in it," said Bonny.

She took away some of the stones. "I can't see any gold," she said. "You were just making it up!"

When they got home the little man had gone. But there were two gold coins on the table, and a note saying, "Keep looking".

Sandy and Bonny did keep looking. They looked every night. But they didn't find the gold.

They are still looking. And they are still arguing!

Reading and writing

Remember!

Choose interesting words for your sentences and labels. Use words from your Word book.

① **What do Sandy and Bonny look like? Write a sentence about each person.**

Sandy   Bonny

② **Answer the questions below.**

- What did Sandy and Bonny argue about?
- What time of day did they hear a tap at the door? Write the sentence that tells you this. Find another sentence that starts in a similar way.
- Who tapped at the door?

③ **Write the adjectives from the text below that describe the old man and what he wore.**

There on the doorstep stood a little man. He wore a green hat and a ragged green coat. His green shoes had holes in the toes.

④ **Change the adjectives to make the man and his clothes different.**

⑤ **Draw the man. Label your drawing.**

76

Reading and writing

Complete the sentences below with the words that Sandy and Bonny said. Copy the sentences.

- "That's funny," he said. "_____

_____."

- "I'll run home _____

_____ ," he said.

- "Suppose someone "_____

_____ ?" he said to himself.

- "_____ !" he shouted.

- "_____ ," said Bonny.

- "_____ !" he said.

Speaking and listening

PAIR WORK. Talk about a time when you argued with someone.

Remember!
Use gestures and body language as well as words to express feelings.

Writing

Write about the time you argued with someone.

1 **Read pages 9 to 15 of the story again. Write the sentences below that are true.**

- Bonny didn't want to share the gold.
- Sandy agreed with Bonny about the gold.
- Bonny put some food and milk on the table.
- Sandy wanted to buy more sheep.
- Bonny wanted to buy new clothes.
- Sandy threw some beans before Bonny threw a chip.
- The little man was hungry so he came downstairs.
- Sandy laughed when Bonny threw water all over the little man.

2 **Join the two sentences to make one sentence. Write the sentences.**

but   because   and

- "We can buy a new house. I can buy lots of new clothes."
- He banged his fist on the table. He was angry.
- The little man came downstairs. He heard loud shouting.
- The little man came downstairs. Sandy and Bonny didn't hear him.
- Bonny threw a jug of water all over the little man. Sandy laughed.

Reading and writing

1 **Copy and complete the sentences below.**

argued   gleaming   evening

- The children _____ over which game to play.
- The candle was _____ in the dark room.
- I went to visit my friend in the _____.

2 **Copy and complete the questions below.**

Who?   Why?

When?   **?**   How?

Where?   What?

Word book

Write these question words in your Word book.

- "<u>Why</u> did you choose a blue car?"
- "_____ rang the doorbell?"
- "_____ will we do today?"
- "_____ is the nearest supermarket?"
- "_____ will the film start?"
- "_____ many children are in the class?"

Remember!

We do not use some nouns in the plural. Examples:

- The man has one **sheep**.
- The woman has ten **sheep**.
- The boy found some **gold**.

3 **Write the compound words from question 2.**

4 **Find two more nouns in the story that we do not use in the plural.**

1 PAIR WORK. Talk about:

- the story the pictures tell.
- how Sandy and Bonny behaved.
- what might have happened when the little man left.

2 Write a new story to match the pictures and tell what happened when the man left.

Thinking time

How can you improve your story? What can you and your partner do to help each other?

9 People who help us

Reading

How do you know this is a non-fiction text?

Read pages 81 to 83 silently, on your own.

Fire! Fire!

Fire keeps us warm and gives us light.

The sun is a giant fire far out in space.

We use fire to cook.

We use fire to keep us warm.

Fireworks make fire to entertain us.

But fire can be dangerous ...
That's why people are trained to be firefighters.
Firefighters put out fires all over the world.

India

China

UK

USA

Japan

Brazil

Kenya

Australia

81

Firefighters put out fires

Sirens ring and lights flash as the fire engine arrives.

The firefighters put out flames with jets of water from hosepipes.

An oil well fire can burn like a huge, flaming torch. This is called a *blowout*.

Firefighters use jet skis to put out fires on small boats. Jet skis work in shallow water.

Big oil tanker fires need fire boats with powerful hoses.

Fires spread quickly through forests. Helicopters water-bomb forest fires.

Helicopters must fly in low.

The forests will grow again.

In the future, giant airships, robots and fast fire-cars might help to put out fires.

Water from airships could put out forest fires.

This robot could fight oil well fires.

This French fire-car might speed through the city streets.

Reading and writing

1 **Copy and complete the sentences below.**

> fireworks   cook   light
> dangerous   firefighters   warm

- Fire keeps us _____ and gives us _____.
- We use fire to _____ food.
- _____ make fire to entertain us.
- Fire can be _____.
- People are trained to be _____.

2 **Find words on page 81 that rhyme with the words in the box. Write the words in rhyming pairs.**

> hire   book   flake
> shy   night

3 **Look at the map on page 81 and answer the questions below.**

- What does UK stand for?
- What does USA stand for?
- What country do you live in? Point to it on the map.

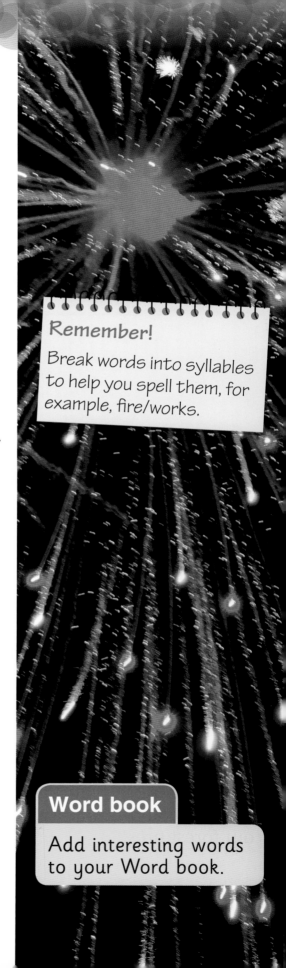

Remember!
Break words into syllables to help you spell them, for example, fire/works.

Word book

Add interesting words to your Word book.

Reading and writing

1 **Read the words in the first box. Then match them to their meanings in the second box.**

| powerful | dangerous | flaming | shallow |

| strong | burning | can hurt you | not deep |

2 **Choose two words from question 1 and write a sentence for each.**

3 **Look at the first picture on page 82. List the clothing and equipment that the firefighter has.**

Speaking and listening

PAIR WORK. Look at the pictures on page 82 and talk about:

- the different places that firefighters put out fires.
- the different places that fires could start on land.
- things that might cause fires on land.

Writing

Write sentences about where firefighters put out fires. Draw and label one of the places.

Reading and writing

Copy and complete the sentences below.

Sirens _____ and lights _____ as the fire engine arrives.

The firefighters put out _____ with jets of _____ from _____.

Speaking and listening

PAIR WORK.

❶ **Talk about:**
- what can cause fires to start in houses.
- what you should do if you notice a fire starting in a house.

❷ **Imagine one of you is making a phone call to report a fire and the other is receiving the call.**
- Who would you phone?
- What number would you call?
- What information would you give?

Writing

❶ **Write the telephone number that you would phone to report a fire.**

❷ **Write a list of the important things you would say when you phone to report a fire.**

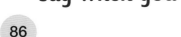

1 Copy and complete the sentences below.

Fires spread quickly through
_____.

_____ water-bomb forest
fires.

Helicopters must _____
in low.

The forests will _____
again.

2 Copy and complete the sentences below.

An oil well _____ can
burn like a huge, flaming
_____.

This is called a _____.

PAIR WORK. Talk about the answers to the questions.

- Why are oil well fires very dangerous to people?
- Why do fires spread quickly through forests?
- Why must the helicopters fly in low at a forest fire?

Reading and writing

1 **Copy and complete the sentences.**

2 **Write a description of the fire boat on page 83.**

> Firefighters use _____ to put out fires on small boats.
>
> Jet skis work in _____ water.
>
> Big oil _____ fires need fire boats with powerful _____.

Speaking and listening

GROUP WORK. Look at the picture of firefighters on a jet ski.

- Talk about the firefighters' clothing and how it differs from a firefighter on land
- Say why it is different.
- Talk about the ways the firefighters' equipment is different to equipment in a fire engine.

❶ Answer the questions below. Use the index to find the page where you will find the answer.

- What kind of fires need fire boats to put out the fire?
- How do helicopters put out forest fires?
- What kind of water do jet skis work in?
- Write the names of two types of fires where hoses are used.
- What warns people that a fire engine is coming?

❷ Choose two things from the index and write a sentence about each.

❸ Read the information about fire again.

- Write a title for a book that has this information.
- Write headings for the different chapters in the book.

Listening and speaking

PAIR WORK. Talk about the pictures.

Why do you think this fire engine has a picture of an aeroplane on it?

Where would you park a fire engine at the airport? Why?

Where would you find fire hydrants?

What are they used for?

Writing

❶ Write a job advertisement for a firefighter.

- Include a list of facts about what a firefighter does.
- Illustrate the advertisement to make it attractive.

❷ Design and label a new piece of equipment for fighting fires in the future.

- Will it travel on land, in the air, at sea or will it be able to fight fires anywhere?

Thinking time

Tell your partner about things that cause fires.

Text acknowledgements
The publishers gratefully acknowledge the permissions granted to reproduce copyright material in the book. Every effort has been made to contact the holders of copyright material, but if any have been inadvertently overlooked, the Publisher will be pleased to make the necessary arrangements at the first opportunity.

Cover illustration: *Kind Emma* Reprinted by permission of HarperCollins*Publishers* Ltd © 2005 Martin Waddell, illustrated by David Roberts. *Jodie the Juggler* Reprinted by permission of HarperCollins*Publishers* Ltd © 2005 Vivian French, illustrated by Beccy Blake; *The Ugly Duckling* Reprinted by permission of HarperCollins*Publishers* Ltd © 2013 James Mayhew; *Kind Emma* Reprinted by permission of HarperCollins*Publishers* Ltd © 2005 Martin Waddell, illustrated by David Roberts; *The Dolphin King* Reprinted by permission of HarperCollins*Publishers* Ltd © 2012 Saviour Pirotta, illustrated by Fausto Bianchi; *World's Deadliest Creatures* Reprinted by permission of HarperCollins*Publishers* Ltd © 2012 Anna Claybourne; If Reprinted by permission of HarperCollins*Publishers* Ltd © 2012 Mij Kelly, illustrated by Mark Beech; *The Pot of Gold* Reprinted by permission of HarperCollins*Publishers* Ltd © 2006 Julia Donaldson, illustrated by Sholto Walker; *Fire! Fire!* Reprinted by permission of HarperCollins*Publishers* Ltd © 2005 Maureen Haselhurst.

We are grateful to the following for permission to reproduce copyright material:
Joyce Vallar for the adapted poem 'Jason the juggler', published in *Hector Hedgehog's Big Book of Rhymes*', copyright © Joyce Vallar; and Robert Charles Howard for the poem 'Dolphin Ballet', published in *Unity Tree: Collected Poems* by Robert Charles Howard, 2007, Createspace, copyright © Robert C. Howard.

In some instances we have been unable to trace the owners of copyright material and we would appreciate any information that would enable us to do so.

Photo acknowledgements
The publishers wish to thank the following for permission to reproduce photographs. Every effort has been made to trace copyright holders and to obtain their permission for the use of copyright materials. The publishers will gladly receive any information enabling them to rectify any error or omission at the first opportunity.

(t = top, c = centre, b = bottom, r = right, l = left)

p7 Larry Maurer/Shutterstock, p12t Blackboard1965/Shutterstock, p12cr Paolo Bona/Shutterstock, p12cl Pete Niesen/Shutterstock, p13t Sergei Bachlakov/Shutterstock, p13cl Mitch Gunn/Shutterstock, p13cr Galina Barskaya/Shutterstock, p13c Diego Barbieri/Shutterstock, p13b Neil Lang/Shutterstock, p14 Paolo Bona/Shutterstock, p18 A_Lesik/Shutterstock, p19 Suzanne Tucker/Shutterstock, p20 Kaliva/Shutterstock, p28 Rido/Shutterstock, p29tr tanya_morozz/Shutterstock p29c LUIS PADILLA_Fotografia/Shutterstock, p29b Cora Mueller/Shutterstock, p31t Ratikova/Shutterstock, p31tc 09196924/Shutterstock, p31tc Gravicapa/Shutterstock, p31bc Dark_Side/Shutterstock, p50 Igor Zh./Shutterstock, p51r imageBROKER/Alamy, p51l Frank Greenaway/Getty Images, p52tl imageBROKER/Alamy Stock Photo, p52cl Helmet Corneli/Alamy Stock Photo, p52tr Michael Patrick O'Neill/Alamy Stock Photo, p52tr Papillo/Alamy Stock Photo, p52c Pat Morris/Ardea, p52cr Marcel an Kammen/Minden Pictures/FLPA, p52bl Ken Griffiths/Shutterstock, p55tc Digital Vision/Getty Images, p53tl Protasov AN/Shutterstock, p53tc ZoonarRF/Shutterstock, p53tr JuniorBildarchiv GmbH/Alamy Stock Photo, p53bl Frank Greenaway/Getty Images, p53br Sirtravelalot/Shutterstock, p54tl Visual&Written SL/Alamy Stock Photo, p54tr imageBROKER/Alamy, p54bl Mark Moffett/Minden Pictures/FLPA, p54br Charles Hood/Avalon, p55t Ken Griffiths/Shutterstock, p55tc Digital Vision/Getty Images, p55bc Protasov AN/Shutterstock, p55b Junior Bildarchiv GmbH/Alamy Stock Photo, p56l Sirtravelalot/Shutterstock, p56c Frank Greenaway/Getty Images, p56r Viaual&Written SL/Alamy Stock Photo, p57c Ludmila Yilmaz/Shutterstock, p57r TTstudio/Shutterstock, p69bl naulicrea/Shutterstock, p69bc Inkley/Shutterstock, p69br Quarta/Shutterstock, p70 Lorelyn Medina/Shutterstock, p81tl Imagetopshop/Alamy, p81tc AAR Studio/Shutterstock, p81tc CandyBox Images/Shutterstock, p81tr Dana.S/Shutterstock, p81 UK: Photofusion Picture Library/Alamy Stock Photo, p81 USA: Nate Allred/Shutterstock, p81 Brazil: AFP/Getty Images, p81 Kenya: Sipa Press/Rex Features, p81 Australia: Evan Collins/Shutterstock, p81 Japan: Tony Myers/Firepix International, p81 China: Tony Myers/Firepix International, p81 India: Pacific Press/Getty Images, p82tl Firepix International, p82tc Naijlah Feanny-Hicks/Corbis, p82tr ChameleonsEye/Shutterstock, p82bl Isaiah Shook/Shutterstock, p82br Getty Images, p83tl Tony Myers/Firepix International, p83cl Bruno Torres/Corbis, p83tr Reuters/Corbis, p83 inset Andrew Brown/Ecoscene/Corbis, p83bl ATG Ltd., p83bc Courtesy of NIST Intelligent Systems Division, p83br Automobiles Peugeot RC, p84 Gary L Jones/Shutterstock p85 etmanee/Shutterstock, p86 Art Konovalov/Shutterstock, p87t Reuters/Corbis, p87b Getty Images, p88 Tony Myers/Firepix International, p89 Imagetopshop/Alamy Stock Photo.